DIARY
OF A LITTLE GIRL
IN OLD NEW YORK

THE AUTHOR AND HER FATHER. FROM AN OLD PHOTO-
GRAPH TAKEN AT BRADY'S DAGUERREAN GALLERY, 10TH ST.
AND BROADWAY, IN 1847.

DIARY
OF A LITTLE GIRL
IN OLD NEW YORK

BY
CATHERINE ELIZABETH HAVENS

APPLEWOOD BOOKS
BEDFORD, MASSACHUSETTS

Diary of a Little Girl in Old New York was first published in 1919.

Thank you for purchasing an Applewood Book. Applewood reprints America's lively classics— books from the past that are still of interest to modern readers. For a free copy of our current catalog, please write to Applewood Books, P.O. Box 365, Bedford, MA 01730.

ISBN 1-55709-524-8

Library of Congress Card Number: 00-110667

TO MY
DEAR NIECES AND NEPHEWS
AND THEIR DESCENDANTS
I DEDICATE THESE MEMOIRS
OF MY CHILDHOOD

FOREWORD

I THINK there are many New Yorkers who, like myself, have spent most of a long life in this delightful old town, that love to go back in memory to the quaint little city of their childhood which has so completely disappeared in the great metropolitan community of to-day.

Perhaps this little book which is a faithful record of events as seen by childhood eyes and recorded in childhood fashion may give an hour or two of pleasure to old friends of the city far and near, and although they may not any more see the tree embowered streets of long ago and the little two-story brick houses with their dormer windows and slanting roofs that used to line both sides of the street, the author hopes that these pages may bring back some of the scenes they were familiar with and help to renew, in spirit at least, some of the old friendships and affections they enjoyed when the heart was young.

DIARY OF A LITTLE GIRL IN OLD NEW YORK

(1849-1850)

August 6, 1849.

I AM ten years old to-day, and I am going to begin to keep a diary. My sister says it is a good plan, and when I am old, and in a remembering mood, I can take out my diary and read about what I did when I was a little girl.

I can remember as far back as when I was only four years old, but I was too young then to keep a diary, but I will begin mine by telling what I can recall of that far-away time.

The first thing I remember is going with my sister in a sloop to visit my aunts, Mrs.

Dering and Mrs. L'Hommedieu, on Shelter Island. We had to sleep two nights on the sloop, and had to wash in a tin basin, and the water felt gritty.

These aunts live in a very old house. It was built in 1733 and is called the Manor House, and some of the floors and doors in it were in a house built in 1635 of wood brought from England.*

The next thing I remember is going with my nurse to the Vauxhall Gardens, and riding in a merry-go-round. These Gardens were in Lafayette Place, near our house, and there was a gate on the Lafayette Place side, and another on the Bowery side.

Back of our house was an alley that ran through to the Bowery, and there was a livery stable on the Bowery, and one time

---

* Note—This house is now in possession of Miss Cornelia Horsford, of Cambridge, Mass., and was the subject of an article by the late Mrs. Martha J. Lamb, in the November number of the Magazine of American History for 1887.—Editor.

2

THE SYLVESTER MANOR HOUSE, SHELTER ISLAND, WHERE MY AUNTS LIVED—BUILT 1733.
NOW IN THE POSSESSION OF MISS CORNELIA HOSFORD, CAMBRIDGE, MASS.

my brother, who was full of fun and mischief, got a pony from the stable and rode it right down into our kitchen and galloped it around the table and frightened our cook almost to death.

Another time he jumped onto a new barrel of flour and went right in, boots and all. He was so mischievous that our nurse kept a suit of his old clothes done up in a bundle, and threatened to put them on him and give him to the old-clothes man when he came along.

The beggar girls bother us dreadfully. They always have the same story to tell, that "my father is dead and my mother is sick, and there's five small children of us, and nary a hapo." The hapo means money.

They come down the steps to the kitchen door and ring the bell and ask for cold victuals; and sometimes they peek through the window into the basement which is

5

my nursery. And one day my brother said to one of them, ''My dear, I am very sorry, but our victuals are all hot now, but if you will call in about an hour they will be cold.'' And she went away awfully angry.

We moved from Lafayette Place to Brooklyn when I was four years old, but only lived there one year. My brother liked Brooklyn because he could go crabbing on the river, but I was afraid of the goats, which chased one of my friends one day. So we came back to New York, and my father bought a house in Ninth Street. He bought it of a gentleman who lived next door to us, and who had but one lung, and he lived on raw turnips and sugar. Perhaps that is why he had only one lung. I don't know.

I am still living in our Ninth Street house. It is a beautiful house and has glass sliding doors with birds of Paradise sitting on palm trees painted on them.

And back of our dining room is a piazza, and a grape vine, and we have lots of Isabella grapes every fall. It has a parlor in front and the library in the middle and the dining room at the back. On the mantel piece in the library is a very old clock that my father brought from France in one of his ships. It has a gilt head of Virgil on the top, and it is all gilt, and stands under a big glass case, and sometimes I watch my father when he takes off the case to wind the clock, and he has to lift it up so high and his hands tremble so, I am afraid he will break it.

Sometimes I think we shall never move again. I think it is delightful to move. I think it is so nice to shut my eyes at night and not to know where anything will be in the morning, and to have to hunt for my brush and comb and my books and my et ceteras, but my mother and my nurse do not feel that way at all.

7

We know a lot of our neighbors who live on Ninth Street. Down near Broadway lives Dr. DeWitt. He is a clergyman, and he and Dr. Chambers and Dr. Knox and Dr. Vermilyea take turns in preaching in the four Dutch Churches. On the corner of University Place lives Mr. James Brown, and above our church on the corner of Tenth Street is Mr. William H. Aspinwall's house, and back of it he has a big picture gallery. On our block on Ninth Street, beginning at University Place on the upper side, is Mr. Jasper Grosvenor, and Mr. Aquilla Stout, and Mr. Cyrus Curtis, and Mr. Henry G. Thompson, and Mr. Cumming, and Mr. Calvin G. How, and Dr. Borrowe. On *our* side of Ninth Street is Mr. Coddington and the Buckners, and on the corner across Fifth Avenue is a big open lot with a high board fence, and next beyond that lives Mr. Quincy, and then Mr. George D. Phelps. Ever so many

8

of the children of these neighbors come to our school. There is another school for girls on our street, kept by Miss Sedgwick.

I forgot to say I have a little niece, nearly as old as I am, and she lives in the country. Her mother is my sister, and her father is a clergyman, and I go there in the summer, and she comes here in the winter, and we have things together, like whooping-cough and scarlatina. Her name is Ellen and she is very bright. She writes elegant compositions, but I beat her in arithmetic. I hate compositions unless they are on subjects I can look up in books.

Beside my little niece, I have a dear cousin near my age. Her father died in New Orleans, and her mother then came to New York to live. She brought all her six children with her, and also the bones of seven other little children of hers, who had died in their infancy. She brought them

9

in a basket to put in the family vault on Long Island.

I think spelling is very funny, I spelt infancy infantsy, and they said it was wrong, but I don't see why, because if my seven little cousins died when they were infants, they must have died in their infantsy; but *infancy* makes it seem as if they hadn't really died, but we just made believe. I have three little sisters who died before I was born and they are buried in the Marble Cemetery, and one day Maggy took me to see their grave, and the cemetery has a high iron railing around it and we had to open a gate and walk through the long grass. The oldest child was named Anna, and she was seven years old, and she went with my oldest sister to Miss McClenahan's school, and she was taken sick in school and my sister brought her home, and she died in forty-eight hours of scarlet fever.

10

My aunt and my cousins came to New
York three years ago. I was in my trun-
dle-bed one night and woke up and saw my
mother putting on her hat and shawl, and
I began to cry, but she told me to be a
good girl and go to sleep, and next day
she would take me to see some little cousins.
So the next day she took me, but first we
went to Mrs. May's toy store, just below
Prince Street on Broadway, to buy some
presents for me to give to my three little
girl cousins. They were living in a nice
house in Bleecker Street, near McDougal
Street, and are named Anna Maria and
Eliza Jane and Sarah Ann.

I took Anna a basket made by some of
the people at the Blind Asylum. It was
made of cloves strung on wire in diamond
shapes, and where the wires crossed there
was a glass bead. She keeps her big copper pennies in it.

Anna is my dearest friend. She and I

11

are together in school, but now they have
moved way up to Fifteenth Street; but I
walk up every morning to meet her and we
walk down to school together.

Sometimes we get some of the big girls'
books, and carry them in our arms, with
the titles on the outside, so the people we
pass will see them. I like to take Miss
D's geometry. There is a Miss Lydia G.
who goes to our school, and she is very
sweet and beautiful, and one day our minister's son was walking to school with her
and carrying her books, and I was just
behind them and I saw him give her a
beautiful red rose, and I guess he was
making love to her and perhaps asking her
to marry him, for she blushed when she
said good-by. He is going to be a clergyman like his father. I hope they will be
happy.

Saturdays I go up to Anna's, and on
Irving Place, between Fourteenth and Fif-

View of Broadway, showing St. Paul's Church, about 1840.

teenth Streets, there is a rope walk, and we like to watch the men walk back and forth making the rope. It is very interesting.[1]

Some Saturdays we go to see our grandmother, who lives with our aunt on Abingdon Square, and she sends Bella her maid out to buy some candy for us, and she tells us about what she did when she lived way down town in Maiden Lane. She is our mother's mother. Anna's parents and my parents were married in the Maiden Lane house, and my father took my mother to his house at 100 Chambers Street to live with him. It was a handsome house, and before they were married, my father took out the wooden mantel pieces, and put in white marble ones to please my mother.

My grandmother's mother lived in Fletcher Street, and she had a sister who lived on Wall Street, opposite the old

---

1 The Academy of Music now stands where the rope walk was.

15

Tontine Coffee-House. They loved each other very much, and were both very sick and expected to die; but my great-grandmother got up off her sick bed and went down to see her sister, and she died there an hour before her sister died, and they were buried together in their brother Augustus Van Horn's vault in Trinity Church Yard. I love to hear my grandmother tell about these old times. She says Mr. R., who married her aunt, was a Tory; which means he was for the English in the Revolutionary War. He was a printer and came from England, and Rivington Street was named for him.

My father's father lived on Shelter Island, and had twenty slaves, and their names were: Africa, Pomp, London, Titus, Tony, Lum, Cesar, Cuff, Odet, Dido, Ziller, Hagar, Judith, and Comas, but my grandfather thought it was wicked to keep slaves, so he told them they could be free, but

16

Tony and Comas stayed on with him.
After he died Tony and Comas had a fight
and Comas cut Tony, and my grandmother
told Tony he must forgive Comas, for the
Bible said "by so doing thou shalt heap
coals of fire on his head," and Tony said,
"Yes, Missy, de nex' time Comas hit me,
I'll heap de coals ob fire on his head and
burn him to a cinder."

Tony and Comas used to make brooms
out of the broom corn, and pound corn into
samp, and send them to my father in New
York by Capt. Mumford's sloop.

New York is getting very big and building up. I walk some mornings with my
nurse before breakfast from our house in
Ninth Street up Fifth Avenue to Twenty-
third Street, and down Broadway home.
An officer stands in front of the House
of Refuge on Madison Square, ready to
arrest bad people, and he looks as if he
would like to find some.

17

Fifth Avenue is very muddy above Eighteenth Street, and there are no blocks of houses as there are downtown, but only two or three on a block. Last Saturday we had a picnic on the grounds of Mr. Waddell's country seat way up Fifth Avenue,[2] and it was so muddy I spoiled my new light cloth gaiter boots. I have a beautiful green and black changeable silk visite,[3] but my mother said it looked like rain and I could not wear it, and it never rained a drop after all. It has a pinked ruffle all around it and a sash behind.

Miss Carew makes my things. She is an old maid, and very fussy, and Ellen and I don't like her. She wears little bunches of curls behind her ears, and when she is cutting out she screws up her mouth, and we try not to laugh, and my mother says

[2] Corner of Thirty-seventh Street and Fifth Avenue, where the Brick Church now stands.—Editor.

[3] A visite was a loose fitting, unlined coat.—Editor.

18

Miss Carew is well born and much thought of and only works for the best families.

There is another person called Miss Platt who comes to sew carpets, and although we don't despise her, which would be very wicked, for my mother says she comes of an excellent old Long Island family, yet Ellen and I don't like to have her use our forks and drink out of our cups. She is very tall and thin and has a long neck that reminds Ellen and me of a turkey gobbler, and her thumb-nails are all flattened from hammering down carpets, and she puts up her front hair in little rings and sticks big pins through them. Ellen and I try to pick out a nicked cup for her to use so that we can recognize it and avoid it.

Mr. Brower makes my shoes and brings them home on Saturday night and stays and tries them on. My sisters go to Cantrell on the Bowery, near Bleecker Street.

19

One time Ellen came down to visit me, and we were both invited to a party at my sister's friend, Mrs. Downer's on 19th Street, and Ellen had not brought her slippers, and so my mother said I must wear my boots, so Ellen would not feel uncomfortable. I did not want to, and asked my sister to persuade her to let me wear my slippers but she only said my mother was perfectly right, so I had to wear my boots.

The wife of one of my brothers thinks I am too fond of pretty clothes, and she sent me a Valentine about a kitten wanting to have pretty stripes like the tiger, and how the tiger told the kitten that she had a great deal nicer life than he did, out in the cold, and that she ought to be contented. I will copy it just as she wrote it. I don't know whether she made it all up, but she made up the verse about me. This is it:

20

A kitten one day,
  In a weak little voice
To a tiger did say:
  "How much I rejoice

"That I am permitted
  In you to behold
One of my own family,
  So great and so bold!

"I'd walk fifty miles, sir,
  On purpose to see
A sight so refreshing
  And pleasant to me!

"With your gay, striped dress,
  You must make a great show,
And be very much courted
  Wherever you go!

"Every beast, great and small,
  In the forest must say,
'I wish I were a tiger,
  So showy and gay!'"

The tiger, half dozing,
  Then opened his eye,
And thus to the kitten
  He deigned a reply.

21

"You envious, foolish
  And weak little thing,
Know that your size, like mine,
  Doth advantages bring.

"Though you have not strength,
  Nor a gay, striped dress,
You have comforts around
  I should love to possess.

"Though I'm powerful and bold,
  I'm the terror of all!
Alas! every one hates me
  And flees at my call.

"You may be very useful
  By catching the mice;
Thus make the folks love you
  And give you a slice

"Of the meat, and a place
  Nice and warm where to sleep,
While, friendless and cold,
  I my wanderings keep!

"Now, envy no more
  Fine looks and gay dress,
But strive to be useful,
  Make happy and bless

22

"The friends who 're around you
    By kindness and care,
And you'll find in return
    Love and happiness there."

*   *   *   *   *

Methinks you, my dear Kitty,
    My tale can explain;
If not, I'll unfold it
    When I see you again.

August 15.

I got so tired doing so much thinking
and writing in my diary that I waited to
think up some more to say.

My father is a very old gentleman. He
was born before the Revolutionary War.
I have three sisters who are nearly as old
as my mother. We have the same father,
but different mothers, so they are not quite
my own sisters; but they say they love
me just the same as if we were own. Two
of them got married and went away to
live with their husbands, but one whose

23

name begins with C is not married. I will call her Sister C in my diary. She has a school. She is educating me.

I love my music lessons. I began them when I was seven years old. Our piano is in the middle room between the parlor and dining-room, and my teacher shuts the sliding doors, and Ellen peeked through the crack to see what I was doing, but she was only six years old.

My teacher is very fond of me. Last year my sister let me play at a big musical party she had, and I played a tune from "La Fille du Regiment," with variations. It took me a good while to learn it, and the people all liked it and said it must be very hard. My mother has had all my pieces bound in a book and my name put on the cover.

I love my music first, and then my arithmetic. Sometimes our class has to stand up and do sums in our heads. Our teacher

24

rattles off like this, as fast as ever she can, "Twice six, less one, multiply by two, add eight, divide by three. How much?" I love to do that.

I have a friend who comes to school with me, named Mary L. She lives on Ninth Street, between Broadway and the Bowery. She and I began our lessons together and sat on a bench that had a little cupboard underneath for our books. She has a nurse named Sarah. Sometimes Ellen and I go there and have tea in her nursery. She has a lot of brothers and they tease us. One time we went, and my mother told us to be polite and not to take preserves and cake but once. But we did, for we had raspberry jam, and we took it six times, but the plates were dolls' plates, and of course my mother meant tea plates. My brother laughed and said we were tempted beyond what we were able to bear, whatever that means. He says it is in the Bible.

25

I hate my history lessons. Ellen likes history because she knows it all and does not have to study her lesson, but one day our teacher asked her to recite the beginning of the chapter, and she had only time to see there was a big A at the heading, and she thought it was about Columbus discovering America and began to recite at a great rate, but the teacher said, "wrong," and it was about Andrew Marvell. Once a girl in our class asked our teacher if what we learned in history was true, or only just made up. I suppose she thought it was good for the mind, like learning poetry.

We don't study spelling any more out of a spelling book. We use the "Scholar's Companion." It has a Latin word at the top and then the English words that come from it, like "Scribere" to write, and below it the noun "Scribe" and the verb to "Scribble." We study Brown's Gram-

26

mar and it has more than 28 rules and I know them all now. And we have finished "Common things" which tells us about Science—why the steam comes out of the kettle, and what makes the clouds, and the rainbow, etc., and now we are going into a harder book called "Familiar Science."

I know a little girl who has a step-mother, and she has one own child, and this step-child, and she dresses her own child very prettily but she makes the step-child wear nankeen pantalettes, and when she plays in the Parade Ground, the boys tease her and call her ginger legs, and she is very unhappy. It is a very sad case.

I meant to write about the time three years ago, when I went with my father to Brady's Daguerrean Gallery, corner of Tenth Street and Broadway, to have our picture taken.

My father was seventy-four, and I was

27

seven. It is a very pretty picture, but people won't believe he isn't my grandfather. He is sitting down and I am standing beside him, and his arm is around me, and my hand hangs down and shows the gold ring on my fore-finger. He gave it to me at New Years to remember him by. I wore it to church and took off my glove so that Jane S., who sits in the pew next to me, would see it, but she never looked at it. We introduced ourselves to each other by holding up our hymn books with our names on the cover, so now we speak. Ellen and I are afraid of the sexton in our church. He looks so fierce and red.

Once in a while my sister takes me down to the Brick Church on Beekman Street, where our family went before I was born. We generally go on Thanksgiving Day. Dr. Spring is the minister. He married my parents and baptized all their children. Mr. Hull is the Sexton, and he puts the

THE BRICK CHURCH, BEEKMAN AND NASSAU STS., WHERE
OUR FAMILY WENT WHEN DR. SPRING WAS MINISTER, AND
WHERE MY PARENTS WERE MARRIED AND ALL THEIR CHIL-
DREN BAPTIZED.

coals in the foot-stoves in the pews. Sometimes the heat gives out and the lady gets up in her pew and waves her handkerchief and Mr. Hull comes and gets her stove and fills it again. When church begins he fastens a chain across the street to keep carriages away.

A man used to stand in front of the pulpit and read two lines of the hymn and start the tune and all the people would sing with him. He had a tuning-fork, and used to snap it and it gave him the key to start the tune on, but that was before I was born. Afterwards they had a choir, and my mother and one of my sisters sang in it one time.

We are a musical family, all except my father; but he went with my sister to hear Jenny Lind in Castle Garden, and when she sang, ''I Know That My Redeemer Liveth,'' the tears ran down his face. My sister took me too, and I heard her sing,

31

"Coming Thro' the Rye" and "John Anderson, My Joe," and a bird song, and she is called the Swedish Nightingale, because she can sing just like one.

September 21.

My parents went up to Saratoga in August for two weeks, to drink the water. They always stay at the Grand Union Hotel. Some time they will take me. It takes my mother a long time to pack, particularly her caps. She has a cold that comes on the nineteenth day every August. She calls it her peach cold, and says it comes from the fuzz on the peaches she preserves and pickles.[4] It lasts six weeks and is very hard to bear. It makes her sneeze and her eyes run, and it is too bad, for she has sweet brown eyes and is very beautiful, and when she was a girl she was called "the pink of Maiden Lane," where she lived.

---

[4] Now known as Hay Fever.—Editor.

This summer I went up to my sister's, my own sister, at Old Church. Maggy, my nurse, took me in a carriage from Hathorn's Livery Stable on University Place, to Catherine Slip on the East River, where we get into a steamboat—sometimes it is the *Cricket,* and sometimes the *Cataline*—and we sail up the sound to the landing where we get off to go to Old Church, and then we get into the stage-coach to ride to my sister's parsonage. I was so wild to get there and to see Ellen and the rest of them that I could hardly wait to have the driver let down the steps for me to get in, and put them up again.

I just love it at Old Church. We play outdoors all day; sometimes in the barn and the hayloft, and sometimes by a brook across the road behind a house where three ladies live who have never married, although they have a vine called Matrimony on their porch, and they are very

33

good to us children and let us run through
their house and yard. On Sundays it is
so quiet we can hear everything they say,
and one morning we heard Miss E. say,
"Ann, do you think it is going to rain?
If I thought it was going to rain I would
take my parasol, but if I thought it was
going to shine I would take my parasol-
ette."

They have a brother Augustus and his
wife Laura who visit them sometimes.
They live in New York, and the sisters
make a great time over their visit. Then
they open their best parlor. It has a thin,
big figured carpet on the floor, and straw
put under it, to make it soft, I guess. One
day a stranger came along and asked the
way to Old Church, and Mr. Augustus
said, "you are right in the heart of the
city." And there are only a few houses.
There is an old Capt. Reid who has a little
house nearby, and he has a music box, and

34

once in a great while we go there to hear it. The three sisters of Mr. Augustus are Charlotte and Angeline and Eliza. Miss Charlotte is going to be married. Miss Angeline has lost some of her teeth, and she keeps little pieces of wax on the mantel piece, and sticks them in when company comes. There are two big square stools covered with black hair cloth in their parlor, and ever so many funny old daguerreotypes standing open on the mantel piece.

Every year there is a fair at the Landing, and of course the minister has to go, and so my sister goes too and takes us. There is an old wagon in the barn beside the carriage, and sometimes we all pile in with my nurse and my sister, and go down to bathe in the salt water. I wish we lived nearer to it and could go in every day.

It is lovely on Sunday at Old Church. My brother-in-law is in the pulpit, and his

35

pew is in the corner of the church, and
there are two pews in front of us. On
pleasant days when the window is open
behind us, we can hear the bees buzzing
and smell the lilac bush; and out on the
salt meadows in front of the church, we
sometimes, alas! hear old Dan F. swear-
ing awfully at his oxen as he is cutting his
salt grass, which it is very wicked of him
to cut on the Sabbath. He has only one
eye and wears a black patch over the other
one, and Ellen and I are afraid of him and
run fast when we pass his house. A nice
gentleman sits in front of us in church and
brings little sugar plums and puts them
on the seat beside him for Katy (Ellen's
sister) to pick up, as she is very little and
it keeps her quiet. One time this gentleman went to sleep in church, and his mouth
was open and Katy had a rose in her little hand and she dropped it into his mouth,
but he did not mind, because she was so
cunning.

THE GOVERNOR'S HOUSE AT NORWALK. . . SOMETIMES HE WOULD DRIVE OVER TO OLD CHURCH TO VISIT MY SISTER AND SEE HIS GRANDCHILDREN.

In the front pew of the three a family
of two parents and three sons and a daughter sit. They are farmers, and they stomp
up the aisle in their big hob-nailed boots,
and the father stands at the door of the
pew and shoves them all in ahead of him
just as he shoos in his hens, and then he
plumps himself down and the pew creaks
and they make an awful noise.

The people in Old Church are very different from our church people in New
York, but my sister says they are very
kind and we must not make fun of them.
Once a year they give her a donation
party, and it is very hard for her for all
the furniture has to be moved to make
room for the people. They bring presents
of hams and chickens and other things.

I could write lots about Old Church and
the good times I have there. My sister's
father-in-law is the Governor of the State,
and sometimes he and his wife drive over

and spend the day with my sister and her
husband, who is their son.   Once when my
sister called us to come and get dressed as
they were going to arrive soon, Ellen said
to me, ''You needn't hurry; he isn't your
grandfather.''   She felt so proud to think
he was the Governor.   But my father is
her grandfather too, and he is much finer
looking than the Governor; and my mother
says she is very proud of my father for he
stands very high in the community—whatever that means.   One time I was very
angry with my father.   It was about the
Ravels.

October 1.

I stopped to get rested a fortnight ago and then I forgot about my diary.

I will now tell about the Ravels. They act in a theater, called Niblo's Theater, and it is corner of Broadway and Prince Street. My biggest own brother goes there with some of his friends to see the plays, and he said he would take me to see the Ravels. But when my father found out about it he would not let me go. He said he did not think it was right for Christians to go to the theater. I went out on our front balcony and walked back and forth and cried so much I hurt my eyes.

Now I must tell about this brother of mine, for he has gone away off to California. He went last February with five other young gentlemen.

When he was twenty-one years old he joined a fire company, and it was called "The Silk Stocking Hose Company" because so many young men of our best families were in it. But they didn't wear their silk stockings when they ran with the engine, for I remember seeing my brother one night when he came home from a fire and he had on a red flannel shirt and a black hat that looked like pictures of helmets the soldiers wear. He took cold and had pain in his leg, and Dr. Washington came and he asked my mother for a paper of pins and he tore off a row and scratched my brother's leg with the pins and then painted it with some dark stuff to make it smart, and it cured him.

Last year my brother had the scarlet fever. His room was on the top floor of our house, and when dear old Dr. Johnston

42

came to see him my mother felt sorry to take him up so many stairs, but he said, "Oh, doctors and hod-carriers can go anywhere." He lives on Fourteenth Street and his daughter comes to school with me.

Last week my sister took me to see Helen R. who is very sick with scarlet fever. They thought she would die, and she was prayed for in school, and now she is getting well. We went up in her room and she looked so funny in bed with all her hair cut off. She lives in Tenth Street.

When my brother was a baby, before I was born, a cousin of my sister came from Buffalo to visit them in our house in Lafayette Place. She came by the Erie Canal, and after she arrived she was taken sick and the doctor said she had the small pox, and she got well. It was very hot weather too. And nobody caught it from her. My sister says when we have a duty to do we will be carried through it, and

43

must not be afraid. All the servants left,
and an old colored woman came to help
who had had the disease. If you are vain
enough to keep your hands from scratching
your face, you won't be marked by it. I
am sure I should be, for I wouldn't want
to have my face all scarred up as long as
I lived.

Before my brother went to California, he
wrote in my album, and this is what he
wrote:

"My sister, thou hast just begun
  To glide the stream of Time,
And as it wafts thee onward
  Towards thy glorious youthful prime,

"Oh, may the fleeting moments
  Which compose thy early years
Be so improved that future days
  Will not look back in tears!"

My album is a beautiful book, bound in
pink kid. I begged one of my brothers

44

(not own) for one, and he gave it to me and wrote lovely poetry on the first page. I don't understand it all, but it sounds like music. I will copy it here in my diary:

"Spotless is the page and bright,
   By heedless fingers yet untarnished;
Ne'er the track of fancy's flight
   Has the virgin leaflet garnished!

"Sweet the impress of the heart
   Stamp'd in words of true affection!
This be every writer's part!
   Love give every pen direction!"

October 15.

My eyes are so bad that I could not write in my diary, and Maggy takes me to Dr. Samuel Elliott's, corner of Amity Street and Broadway, and he puts something in that smarts awfully. He has two rooms, and all the people sit in the front room, waiting, and his office is in the back room; and they have black patches over their eyes

—some of them—and sit very quiet and solemn. On each side of the folding doors are glass cases filled with stuffed birds and I know them all by heart now and wish he would get some new ones.

When I was four years old I had my tonsils cut out by Dr. Horace Green, who lives on Clinton Place. My nurse asked him to give them to her, so he put them in a little bottle of alcohol and sealed it up, and she keeps it in the nursery closet, and sometimes she shows it to me to amuse me, but it doesn't, only I don't like to hurt her feelings. My grandmother gave me a five-dollar gold piece for sitting so still when they were cut out.

November 8.

My diary has stopped on account of my eyes, and I have not studied much.

Ellen is here, and we have had fun. We have been down to Staten Island to one of my sisters. She has ice cream on Thurs-

days, so we try to go then. One day I ate
it so fast is gave me a pain in my forehead,
and my brother-in-law said I must warm
it over the register, and I did, and it all
melted, and then they all laughed and
said he was joking, but they gave me some
more.

My brother-in-law is a dear old gentleman, but he is very deaf. He has a lovely
place and every kind of fruit on it, and
there is a fountain in front with pretty
fish in it. The farmer's name is Andrew,
and when he goes to market, Ellen and I
go with him in the buggy; and we always
ask him to take us past Polly Bodine's
house. She set fire to a house and burned
up ever so many people, and I guess she
was hung for it, because there is a wax
figure of her in Barnum's Museum.

Maggy takes us there sometimes, and it
is very instructive, for there are big glasses
to look through, and you can see London

and Paris and all over Europe, only the
people look like giants, and the horses as
big as elephants. Once we stayed to see
the play. Maggy says whenever the statue
on St. Paul's Church hears the City Hall
Clock strike twelve, it comes down. I am
crazy to see it come down, but we never
get there at the right time.

My mother remembers when the City
Hall was being built; and she and Fanny
S. used to get pieces of the marble and
heated them in their ovens and carried
them to school in their muffs to keep their
hands warm. She loves to tell about her
school days, and I love to hear her.
December 10.

My eyes are better and I will write a
little while I can.

Ellen and I went out shopping alone.
We went to Bond's dry-goods store on
Sixth Avenue, just below Ninth Street, to
buy a yard of calico to make an apron for

48

My mother remembers when the City Hall was being built; and she and Fanny Sharp used to get pieces of the marble and heated them in their ovens and carried them to school in their muffs to keep their hands warm.

Maggy's birthday. We hope she will like it. It is a good quality, for we pulled the corner and twitched it as we had seen our mothers do, and it did not tear. Ellen and I call each other Sister Cynthia and Sister Juliana, and when we bought the calico, Ellen said, "Sister Cynthia, have you any change? I have only a fifty-dollar bill papa left me this morning," and the clerk laughed. I guess he knew Ellen was making it up!

Sometimes we play I am blind and Ellen leads me along on the street, and once a lady went by and said to her little girl, "See that poor child, she is blind," and perhaps when I get old I may be really blind as a punishment for pretending. But once Maggy was walking behind us, and she called out, "Hurry, children, don't walk so slow," only she always called us by our names out loud, Katy and Ellen. I don't think grown-up people understand

what children like—we love to dress up in
long frocks, and I guess all little girls like
to, for my mother did. When she was
about twelve years old she put on her
mother's black lace shawl and walked out
on Broadway in it, and her cousin, Katy
Lawrence, met her in front of St. Paul's
Church and saw the shawl dragging on
the sidewalk and my mother looking behind to see if it dragged, and she told my
grandmother about it, and my mother was
punished. I know it was wrong, but it
must have been lovely to think that it
really dragged and that people were looking at it. I am afraid I should have for-
gotten it was wrong, but I don't know, for
we all have an inward monitor, my sister
says.

There is a bakery kept by a Mr. Walduck
on the corner of Sixth Avenue and Eighth
Street, and they make delicious cream puffs,
and when I have three cents to spare, I

run down there right after breakfast, before school begins, and buy one and eat it there.

On the corner of Broadway and Ninth Street is a chocolate store kept by Felix Effray, and I love to stand at the window and watch the wheel go round. It has three white stone rollers and they grind the chocolate into paste all day long. Down Broadway, below Eighth Street is Dean's candy store, and they make molasses candy that is the best in the city. Sometimes we go down to Wild's, that is way down near Spring Street, to get his iceland moss drops, good for colds.

My mother says Stuart's candy store down on Greenwich and Chambers Streets used to be the store in her day. When she was a little girl in 1810, old Kinloch Stuart and his wife Agnes made the candy in a little bit of a back room and sold it in the front room, and sometimes they used to

let my mother go in and stir it. After
they died their sons, R. and L. Stuart, kept
up the candy store in the same place, and
it is there still.

When my mother lived at 19 Maiden
Lane, Miss Rebecca Bininger and her
brother lived across the way from her, and
they had a store in the front of their home
and sold fine groceries, and their sitting
room was behind the store. They were
Moravians and they used to ask my mother
sometimes to come over and sing hymns to
them, and my mother says they were so
clean and neat that even their pot-hooks
and trammels shone like silver, and by and
by Miss Rebecca would go into the store
and my mother would hear paper rustling,
and Miss Rebecca would come back and
bring her a paper filled with nuts and
raisins for a present.

Sometimes my mother gives us a shilling
to go and get some ice cream. We can get

a half plate for sixpence, and once Ellen
dared to ask for a half plate with two
spoons, and they gave it to us, but they
laughed at us, and then we each had three
cents left. That was at Wagner's, on the
other side of Broadway, just above Eighth
Street. There is another ice cream saloon
on the corner of Broadway and Waverly
Place, called Thompson's.

I hope Ellen will stay all winter. She
is full of pranks, and smarter than I am
if she is younger, and I hope we will have
lots of snow. When there is real good
sleighing, my sister hires a stage sleigh
and takes me and a lot of my schoolmates
a sleigh ride down Broadway to the Battery and back. The sleigh is open and
very long; and has long seats on each side,
and straw on the floor to keep our feet
warm, and the sleigh bells sound so cheer-
ful. We see some of our friends taking

55

their afternoon walk on the sidewalk, and I guess they wish they were in our sleigh!

Stages run through Bleecker Street and Eighth Street and Ninth Street right past our house, and it puts me right to sleep when I come home from the country to hear them rumble along over the cobblestones again. There is a line on Fourteenth Street too, and that is the highest uptown.

I roll my hoop and jump the rope in the afternoon, sometimes in the Parade Ground on Washington Square, and sometimes in Union Square. Union Square has a high iron railing around it, and a fountain in the middle. My brother says he remembers when it was a pond and the farmers used to water their horses in it. Our Ninth Street stages run down Broadway to the Battery, and when I go down to the ferry to go to Staten Island, they go through Whitehall Street, and just opposite the

56

Bowling Green on Whitehall Street, there is a sign over a store, "Lay and Hatch," but they don't sell eggs.

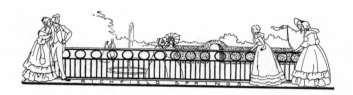

January 2, 1850.

Yesterday was New Year's Day, and I had lovely presents. We had 139 callers, and I have an ivory tablet and I write all their names down in it. We have to be dressed and ready by ten o'clock to receive. Some of the gentlemen come together and don't stay more than a minute; but some go into the back room and take some oysters and coffee and cake, and stay and talk. My cousin is always the first to come, and sometimes he comes before we are ready, and we find him sitting behind the door, on the end of the sofa, because he is bashful. The gentlemen keep dropping in all day and until long after I have gone to bed; and the horses look tired, and the livery men make a lot of money.

Mr. Woolsey Porter and his brother, Mr. Dwight Porter always come in the evening and sit and talk a long time. They are very fond of one of my sisters. They keep a school for boys in 13th Street, and it is called Washington Institute, and one of my brothers goes to it. Mr. William Curtis Noges is another gentleman who always comes and stays awhile, and he calls us ''cousin,'' but we are not real cousins.

Next January we shall be half through the nineteenth century. I hope I shall live to see the next century, but I don't want to be alive when the year 2000 comes, for my Bible teacher says the world is coming to an end then, and perhaps sooner.

January 14.

My mother said she could not afford to get me another pair of kid gloves now,

but my sister took me down to Seaman
and Muir's, next door to the hospital on
Broadway, and bought me a pair. I like
salmon color, but she said they would not
be useful. Strang and Adriance is next
door to Seaman and Muir's and we go
there sometimes.

We get our stockings and flannels at S.
and L. Holmes' store, near Bleecker Street.
They are two brothers and they keep German cologne. Rice and Smith have an
elegant store on the corner of Waverly
Place, and they keep German cologne too.
We go sometimes to Stewart's store, way
down on the corner of Chambers Street,
but I like best to go to Arnold and Con-
stable's on Canal Street, they keep elegant
silks and satins and velvets, and my mother
always goes there to get her best things.
She says they wear well and can be made
over for me or for Ellen sometimes.

My Staten Island sister gave me a nice

PORTRAIT OF LITTLE MISS PLYMPTON AND HER BROTHER, SHOWING THE QUAINT STYLE OF CHILDREN'S ATTIRE IN THE DAYS OF OUR GRANDMOTHERS. — EDITOR.

silk dress, only it is a soft kind that does not rustle. I have a green silk that I hate, and the other day I walked too near the edge of the sidewalk, and one of the stages splashed mud on it, and I am so glad, for it can't be cleaned.

On Canal Street, near West Broadway, is a box store, where my mother goes for boxes. They have all kinds, from beautiful big band boxes for hats and long ones for shawls, down to little bits of ones for children, and all covered with such pretty paper.

Maggy, my nurse, is a very good woman, and reads ever so many chapters in her Bible every Sunday, and she said one day, ''Well, Moses had his own troubles with these Children of Israel.'' I suppose she was thinking about the troubles she has with us children. I have a little bit of a hymn book that was given to one of my sisters (not own) ''by her affectionate

63

mother.'' It was printed in 1811 and is called ''The Children's Hymn Book,'' and some of the hymns are about children sleeping in church, and they are very severe, and I don't have to learn them, but Maggy teaches me some pretty verses sometimes to sing. I will copy down one of the hymns about sleeping in church. It is called ''The sin and punishment of children who sleep in the House of God.'' This is the hymn:

Sleeper awake! for God is here
Attend his word, his anger fear;
For while you sleep his eyes can see,
His arm of power can punish thee.

This day is God's, the day He blest,
His temple this, His holy rest;
And can you here recline your head,
And make the pew or seat your bed?

Jehovah speaks, then why should you
Shut up your eyes and hearing too?
In anger He might stop your breath,
And make you sleep the sleep of death!

Dear children then of sleep beware!
To hear the sermon be your care;
For if you all God's message mind,
For sleep no season will you find.

Remember Eutychus of old,
He slept while Paul of Jesus told;
In sleep he fell, in Acts 'tis said,
That he was taken up for dead.

Hear this ye sleepers and be wise,
And shut no more your slumbering eyes,
For 'tis an awful truth to tell
That you can never sleep in Hell!

There is another hymn called Hell, but
my mother does not like me to learn it.
She thinks it is too severe. We use the
book "Watt's & Select" in our church, and
I know lots of them. It is the University
Place Church. There is one hymn I have
learnt, and in it, it says:

Like young Abijah may I see
That good things may be found in me.

and my sister says when she was a little
girl and learned it, she always thought
that when Abijah died, they cut him open
and found sugar plums in him.

Sometimes when the sermon is very long,
Ellen and I count the bonnets, to keep ourselves awake. She chooses the pink ones
and I take the blue, and she generally gets
the most, but some ladies wear lovely white
ones of uncut velvet. Last winter I had
a gray beaver, faced with cherry colored
satin, and it had a row of narrow cherry
colored satin ribbon rosettes like a wreath
around it, and cherry colored satin strings
to tie it under my chin, and I had a plaid
woolen coat, and gray and white furs, and
I left the muff in Randolph's book store,
and when I went back for it, some one had
taken it, and I never got it again.

January 20.

Last Sunday my mother let me go with
Maggy to her church. It is called the

Scotch Seceders' Church. Mr. Harper is the minister. The church is in Houston Street. In the pew were her father and mother. They live in Greenwich village, and once she took me there, and her mother gave me elegant bread and butter with brown sugar thick on it.

Maggy has a sister married to a weaver, and his name is George Ross, and he is growing rich by buying land and selling it, and soon he is to be an alderman. Her other sister is Matilda, and she is my sister's maid. Our other servants are colored people. The man waiter is colored, and we hear him asking our cook on Sunday if she is going to Zion or to Bethel to church, and her name is Harriet White, but she is very black.

We have a Dutch oven in our kitchen beside the range, and in the winter my mother has mince pies made, and several baked at once, and they are put away and

heated up when we want one. My mother
makes elegant cake, and when she makes
rich plum cake, like wedding cake, she
sends it down to Shaddle's on Bleecker
Street to be baked.

January 25.

This is my mother's birthday and my
grandmother came to dinner. My mother
is forty-nine to-day, and I hope she will
live to be a hundred. She has a lovely
voice and sings old songs, and plays them
herself.

She went to a big school in Litchfield
kept by a Miss Pierce, but was only there
three months. Her father thought it was
too cold for her to stay there. While she
was there she boarded at Dr. Lyman
Beecher's and his wife died and her coffin
stood below the pulpit, and he preached
her funeral sermon, and my mother heard
him. She says a Mr. Nettleton came there
to preach once, and at breakfast he and

Dr. Beecher had mugs of cider with pearlash in it, and they heated a poker and put it in the cider to make it fizz. It must have been horrid.

My oldest aunt went to Miss Pierce's school, and got acquainted with a young gentleman who was at Judge Gould's Law School in Litchfield, and she married him in 1811, and he became a clergyman, and Queen Victoria ordered him to come to Edinburgh to try to get an estate. That was in 1837. He took my aunt and their children and went away in a ship, and it took them ninety days to cross the Atlantic Ocean, and when they get the estate they will live in the castle, and my mother and I will go and visit them.

My aunt was sixteen and my uncle was nineteen when they were married, and he was born in Beaufort in South Carolina, and had a good deal of money. I do hope they will live in the castle! This is called a law suit they are having to get the estate.

This aunt took dancing lessons when she was a girl of Mr. Julius Metz, and she danced the shawl dance, and was very graceful, and she and my mother took music lessons on the piano, of Mr. Adam Geib, and he played the organ in Trinity Church, and he and his brother, George Geib, sold pianos. A young lady in Edinburgh told one of my Scotch cousins that she supposed all the Americans were copper colored, and he said, "Well, you know my father is a Scotchman, so that is why I am white."

February 14.

I have had a lot of Valentines to-day.

Once when I was six years old I teased one of my brothers (not own) for a valentine, and he sent me one written on a sheet of lovely note paper with a rose bud in the corner. It is pretty long to copy, and

I don't know all it means, but it sounds
tinkly, like music.   This is it:

Little Kitty one day,
In her wheedling way,
With her kisses and smiles
And twenty such wiles,
   Did a valentine request;
That somehow or other
My brain I should bother
And verses indite
In stupidity's spite,
   To comply with her simple behest.

Now, though it may seem
   But a trifling affair
To fill up a ream
   Of paper so fair
      With words that will jingle in rhyme,
Yet to put them together
   In proper connection
And give them a meaning
   And useful direction
      Wit is quite as essential as time.

71

And here, little Kitty,
  Will please to observe
That speech, to be witty,
  Must ever deserve
    The aids of reflection and sense;
And careless, gay prattle
  And voluble talk,
Though making much rattle
  Will scarcely be thought
    Very witty or worthy defense!

But as verse that is fired
  With passion and truth,
From a fancy inspired
  By beauty and worth,
    Hath a charm that no heart can resist,
So the thoughts of a mind
  That's calm, clear and pure,
When they utterance find,
  In words plain and sure,
    Are generally reckoned the best!

This brother is a lawyer, and now he
has gone to California too, to a place called
Eureka. He has a lovely voice, and so

has my own brother too, who went to California last year, and they used to sing rounds with my sister.

When my mother sings one of her songs, she has to cross her left hand over her right on the piano to play some high notes, and make what my teacher says is "a turn," and it is beautiful. This song is called "The Wood Robin," and another one begins, "Come, rest in this bosom, my own stricken deer." My mother knows ever so many songs, and some of them were sung before she was born. One of them is called "The Maid of Lodi," and another is "The Old Welsh Harper," and another, "A Social Dish of Tea," and a lot of others.

April 12.

I have a school mate who lives across the street, and her name is Minnie B. Her father is a doctor, and she has a brother, Sam, and he is fifteen years old and big,

73

and to-day I ran over to see her, and Sam opened the front door, and when he saw me, he picked me up in his arms to tease me, but he didn't see his aunt Sarah who was coming downstairs, and when she saw him she was very severe, and said, "Samuel, put that child down right away, and come and eat your lunch." I don't dislike Sam, but I think he was very rude to-day, and I am glad his aunt Sarah made him behave himself.

Minnie B. and Lottie G., who live on the corner of University Place and Ninth Street, and Mary P., who lives on Ninth Street across Fifth Avenue, and I have a sewing society, and we sew for a fair, but we don't make much money.

But four years ago there was a dreadful famine in Ireland, and we gave up our parlor and library and dining room for two evenings for a fair for them, and all my schoolmates and our friends made things,

74

No. 12.

A most useful art.

PEN-MAN-SHIP = PENMANSHIP.

No 29.

Good advice for the rude.

BE-SIEVE-ILL = BE CIVIL.

TWO OF MY BROTHER'S CHARADES MADE FOR THE FAIR
HELD IN OUR LIBRARY FOR THE BENEFIT OF THE IRISH
FAMINE SUFFERERS.

and we sent the poor Irish people over three hundred dollars. My brothers made pictures in pen and ink, and called them charades, and they sold for fifty cents apiece; like this: a pen, and a man, and a ship, and called it, ''a desirable art'' Penmanship. The brother who used to be so mischievous, is studying hard now to be an engineer and build railroads. He draws beautiful bridges and aqueducts.

One Fourth of July, my father got a carriage from Hathorn's stable and took my mother and my sister and my brother and me out to see the High Bridge. It is built with beautiful arches, and brings the Croton water to New York. My brother says he remembers riding to the place where the Croton aqueduct crossed Harlem River by a syphon before the Bridge was built, and the man who took charge of it opened a jet at the lowest point, and sent a two-inch stream up a hundred feet.

77

My mother says when she was young,
everybody drank the Manhattan water.
Everybody had a cistern for rain water for
washing, in the back-yards. And when
she lived in Maiden Lane, the servants had
to go up to the corner of Broadway and
get the drinking water from the pump
there. It was a great bother, and so when
my grandfather built his new house at 19
Maiden Lane, he asked the aldermen if he
might run a pipe to the kitchen of his house
from the pump at the corner of Broadway,
and they said he could, and he had a
faucet in the kitchen, and it was the first
house in the city to have drinking water
in it, and after that several gentlemen
called on my grandfather and asked to see
his invention. My mother says the Manhattan water was brackish and not very
pleasant to drink.

My grandfather had ships that went to
Holland and he brought skates home to

78

THE STONE BRIDGE AT BROADWAY AND CANAL ST. MY GRANDFATHER USED TO SAY TO HIS CHILDREN THAT WHOEVER WAS UP EARLY ENOUGH IN THE MORNING COULD RIDE WITH HIM IN HIS GIG AS FAR AS THE STONE BRIDGE.

his children, and they used to skate on
the Canal that is now Canal Street and on
the pond where the Tombs is now, and my
mother says that the poor people used to
get a rib of beef and polish it and drill
holes in it and fasten it on their shoes to
skate on. The Canal ran from Broadway
to the North River, and had a picket fence
on both sides of it, and there were only
three houses on its side, and they were
little white wooden houses with green
blinds. My grandfather used to tell his
children that whichever one would be up
early enough in the morning could ride
with him before breakfast in his gig as far
as the stone bridge, and that was the bridge
at Canal Street and Broadway.

My grandfather bought the lot for his
new house from Mr. Peter Sharp, the father
of my mother's schoolmate, Fanny. The
lot was 28 feet wide, but the house was
only 25 feet wide, and there was an alley

3 feet wide that was used by the shop people to get to the kitchen at the back of the house.

This Mr. Sharp was an alderman and he was a Democrat, and my grandfather was a Federalist, and they used to exchange their newspapers so as to read both kinds, and sometimes when my mother was waiting for Fanny to go to school, at her house, Mr. Sharp would throw down the paper and say a very wicked word about the Federalists. Another alderman is Mr. John Yates Cebra, a cousin of my mother's. He lives on Cebra Avenue on Staten Island, and once I went there with my sister in her barouche and the grays. The grays are beautiful horses.

May 15.

I meant to tell in my diary that my sister taught me to sew when I was five years old, and to darn little holes in a stocking, and she thought I was funny to want to

do the biggest hole first, but I did, so as
to get done with it. She gives me the
skeins of sewing silk to wind, and I love
to get the knots out of them.

When my mother was a little girl she
used to go from her house at 84 Beekman
Street to Fletcher Street every Saturday,
to stay over Sunday at her Grandfather
Cebra's, but before she went she had to
do some hemming in the morning and do
it neat and nice, or her mother would rip
it out and make her do it over again. Her
Aunt Peggy lived with her grandfather,
and when she took my mother out to walk,
there were only four policemen in New
York then, and they were called Constables.
They carried a stick like a broomstick,
painted white and going up to a gilt point
with a blue ribbon at the top, and they
knew who everybody was, and used to say,
''Good evening, Miss Peggy, and how is
your father to-night?'' My mother's

83

grandfather was an episcopalian, and had
a pew in Trinity Church, and it was so
cold that her Aunt Peggy carried a big
martin muff and put my mother's little
feet in it to keep them warm. And she
remembers old Bishop Hobart, and says he
wore his hair in a queue, and spectacles
with big brown wooden rims. But my
mother's father was a presbyterian and
went to the Brick Church, and he joined
it when he saw some poor black men go up
to the communion table while he sat still
in his pew, and he felt he was very wicked.
He died in 1817, and a Mr. Jarvis came
and took a plaster cast of his face and then
painted a portrait from it, and my Aunt
took it with her when she went to live
in Edinburgh in Scotland. Mr. Jarvis
painted portraits of my cousin Annie's
father and mother too in New Orleans.

My grandfather had a ship called the
Snow, and he used to tell people he had

84

seen *Snow* in June more than three feet
deep, and they thought he meant a snow
storm, and they wouldn't believe him, but
he only meant his ship. He was full of
fun. My own father had ships, too, as well
as my mother's father. And he gave some
of his ships to our Government for them to
use in the War of 1812. And one of them
was called the *General Armstrong,* and
the Captain was Samuel Chester Reid.
And he was a very brave man, and he
took his ship into the harbor of Fayal in
the Azores Islands, to get some drinking
water, and three British ships saw our
ship and they fought us, and when Captain Reid saw he could not beat them because they had so many more men and
guns than he had, he sank the *General
Armstrong,* and all this fight kept the
British from getting to the Gulf of Mex-
ico in time to help the ships that were
waiting for them, and so the fight helped

85

to bring the War of 1812 to an end. This is all told in our American History book. And my father ought to be paid money by our government, and he sent Captain Reid to Washington to try to get it a few years ago, but President Polk would not let him have it—but they gave Captain Reid a sword because he was so brave.

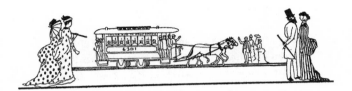

July 15.

I have not written in my diary for ever
so long, but now school has just closed for
the summer, and I have more time.

We had a new study last winter, something to strengthen our memories. The
teacher was a Miss Peabody from Boston,
and she has a sister married to a Mr. Na-
thanial Hawthorne, who writes beautiful
stories.

We had charts to paint on, and stayed
after school to paint them, and one-half of
the page was a country and the other half
was for the people who lived in that country, and the country was painted one color,
and the people another color, and this is
the way it will help us to remember; for

Mesopotamia was yellow, and Abraham, who lived there, was royal purple, and so I shall never forget that he lived in Mesopotamia, but I may not remember after all which was yellow, the man or the country, but I don't suppose that is really any matter as long as I don't forget where he lived. We did not study it long, but it was fun to stay and paint after school.

Professor Hume teaches us natural science, and every Wednesday he lectures to us, and one day he brought the eye of an ox and took it all apart and showed us how it was like our own eyes. And another time he brought an electric battery, and we joined our hands, ever so many of us, and the end girl took hold of the handle of the battery, and we all felt the shock, and it tingled and pricked.

Sometimes he talks on chemistry, and brings glass jars and pours different things into them and makes beautiful colors. He told us we could always remember the seven colors of the rainbow by the word, v i b g y o r.

Professor Edwardes has been teaching us French. He is a little bit of a man, with a big head, and gray hair and a broken nose, and when he recites one of La Fontaine's Fables, he says, "L'animal vora-a-ace," and rolls up his eyes until you can only see the whites of them. Mr. Roy comes from the Union Seminary on University Place, to teach us Latin.

Mr. Dolbear used to teach us writing, but now we have Mr. Hoogland. He wears blue spectacles and is very kind, and sometimes gives us 4 which is the mark for perfect, when we don't deserve it. One day he was behind a row of desks next to the wall, and one of the girls pulled the chair out from under him, and down he went between two desks. It was a very cruel thing to do, but perhaps she did not

mean to, but I'm afraid she did. I won't
tell her name. Both Mr. Dolbear and Mr.
Hoogland can take their pen and make a
few flourishes, and it will be a beautiful
swan or an eagle on the outside of our
copy books.

August 6.

This is my birthday again, and I am now
eleven years old. School will begin again
in September and so I will write some more
in my diary while I have time.

I think I will tell about the school my
mother went to.

The first school she went to was in Fair
Street, and that is now Fulton Street, east
of Broadway. It was kept by a Mrs. Mer-
rill, an old lady who took a few little children, and each child brought her own little chair.

Then my mother went to Mr. Pickett's,
and she says that was *the* school of that
time. He had two sons who taught in

the school. I will tell about it just as she has written it down for me.

"The school at first was at 148 Chambers Street, on the south side near Greenwich Street. Mr. Pickett's residence was in front and the school buildings were in the yard behind, running up three stories, with a private side entrance for the scholars, and a well in the yard. The house was brick, painted yellow, but the school buildings were of wood. The first and second floors were for the boys, and the third for the girls, beautifully fitted up, and hardwood floors. On the wall in the four corners of the girls' room were oval places painted blue, and on them in gilt letters were inscribed, Attention, Obedience, Industry, Punctuality. Mr. Pickett's desk was in the center of the room. The desks were painted mahogany color, and put in groups of four, facing each other. Wooden benches without backs were screwed to the floor. On top of the desks were little frames with glass fronts for the copies for writing, and the copies were slid in at the sides. Some of them were, Attention to study, Beauty soon decays, Command yourself, Death is inevitable, Emulation is noble, Favor is deceitful, Good Humor pleases, et cetera. Quill pens were used, which Mr. Pickett made himself.''

Some of the girls who went to school with my mother had awfully funny long names. One was Aspasia Seraphina Imogene and her last name was Bogardus.

She had ten brothers and sisters, and these were some of their names: Maria Sabina, Wilhelmina Henrietta, Laurentina Adaminta, Washington Augustus, Alonzo Leonidas Agamemnon, Napoleon LePerry Barrister. There were eleven children, and their mother named them after people she had read about in novels. It must

have been funny to hear their nurse call
them all to come to dinner.

My name is Catherine Elizabeth. I
don't like it very much. It makes me
think of Henrietta Maria and Marie An-
toinette and all those old queens with long
names we study about in history, but my
mother calls me Katy, and sometimes
Katrintje, which is the Dutch for "little
Katy."

Some other schools in New York now
are Mme. Canda's on Lafayette Place, Mme.
Okill's on Eighth Street, Mme. Chegary's,
the Misses Gibson on the east side of Union Square, Miss Green's on Fifth Avenue,
just above Washington Square, and Spingler Institute on the west side of Union
Square, just below Fifteenth Street. On
the corner of Fifteenth Street next to
Spingler Institute is the Church of the
Puritans. Dr. Cheever is the minister, and
he and the church people are called a long

93

name, which means that they think slavery is wicked, and they help the black slaves that come from the South, to get to Canada where they will be free.

N. B.—My mother has read my diary and corrected the spelling, and says it is very good for a little girl. She has written down her memories of old New York, for me, and she was born in 1801, and can remember back to 1805, some things.

FOURTEENTH STREET, BETWEEN FIFTH AND SIXTH AVENUES, SHOWING THE OLD SPINGLER FARMHOUSE JUST BACK OF THE PRESENT SPINGLER BUILDING ON UNION SQUARE.

RULES OF MY SISTER'S SCHOOL
FOR YOUNG LADIES

These rules were read aloud to the assembled scholars—from 80 to 90 in number usually—once a year only, at the opening of the school in September.—Editor.

1. Every young lady must be in her seat at 9 o'clock with the Bible in her hand, in readiness for the opening exercises of the school. Each one should bow her head in a reverential manner during prayer.

2. Each scholar is desired to familiarize herself with the course of study, that immediately after the opening of the school, she may commence preparation for her first recitation. All unnecessary questions both to teachers and scholars may thus be avoided.

3. All talking and laughing, note writing, conversation by signs, eating, and leaving of seats, are entirely forbidden during study and recitation hours.

97

4. Loud conversation, romping, or rudeness of manner must not in any case be indulged in, during the recess. This rule applies also to entering the house in the morning and leaving it after school.

5. Perfect neatness in person is expected of every young lady. No papers or crumbs must be thrown upon the floor. No pencil or other marks must be made upon any part of the house. Desks must not be cut or injured by marks or otherwise, and they must be arranged in perfect order. Books should be carefully covered and carefully used, and not left to lie upon the outside of the desk at any time.

6. In passing to recitations the young lady who sits nearest the door will go first, and in returning the same rule will be observed.

7. No tardiness at school, or failure in

lessons, will be excused, or permission given to leave before the close of school, except by a written note from one of the parents of the young lady.

8. For every perfect lesson the scholar will receive four good marks. Two entire failures in answering, or general imperfect answers, will incur a forfeit mark.

9. Good marks will be given for punctuality, neatness, order, and general excellence, and disgrace marks will be incurred for tardiness, disorder, improper manners, deficiency in studies, and want of amiability.

10. At the end of each month, the marks will be counted so that each one may know her standing in her classes. Reports will then be sent to the parents.

11. School will close at a few minutes before 2 o'clock, and when the bell is rung, the young ladies may arrange their books

silently for leaving, and remain at their places until they receive permission to leave, and then the young lady who sits nearest the door in each class may lead the way.

12. Finally, we desire that the rules of politeness and good breeding observed in the best regulated society, will uniformly be practiced here. And as the Bible is the great rule of duty, for both teachers and scholars, so it is hoped that that truth and virtue and christian kindness and courtesy, which it inculcates, will, at all times, be the governing principle of conduct to all the members of this school.

THE WOOD ROBIN

A Song of the Eighteenth Century

Stay, sweet enchanter of the grove,
  Leave not so soon thy native tree,
Oh, warble still those notes of love,
  While my fond heart responds to thee!

Rest thy soft bosom on the spray,
  Till chilly Autumn frowns severe,
Then charm me with thy parting lay,
  And I will answer with a tear.

But soon as Spring, enriched with flowers,
  Comes dancing o'er the new drest plain,
Return and cheer thy native bowers,
  My robin, with thy notes again!

CPSIA information can be obtained
at www.ICGtesting.com
Printed in the USA
BVHW01s1927191217
503241BV00001B/3/P